Taste of
CHRISTMAS

Fruitcake
& Other Seasonal Favorites Cookbook

COOKBOOK

Recipes and Holiday Inspiration

© 2014 by Barbour Publishing, Inc.

Written and compiled by MariLee Parrish.

Print ISBN 978-1-62836-878-9

All rights reserved. No part of this publication may be reproduced or transmitted for commercial purposes, except for brief quotations in printed reviews, without written permission of the publisher.

All scripture quotations are taken from the King James Version of the Bible.

Published by Barbour Books, an imprint of Barbour Publishing, Inc., P.O. Box 719, Uhrichsville, Ohio 44683, www.barbourbooks.com

Our mission is to publish and distribute inspirational products offering exceptional value and biblical encouragement to the masses.

Member of the
Evangelical Christian
Publishers Association

Printed in the United States of America.

Taste of
CHRISTMAS

Fruitcake
& Other Seasonal Favorites Cookbook

COOKBOOK

Recipes and Holiday Inspiration

BARBOUR BOOKS
An Imprint of Barbour Publishing, Inc.

It seems to us that some people should stop
trampling upon the delicious fruitcake
and enjoy a bite.

UNKNOWN

 # Contents

Fruitcake is a Christmas tradition that is timeless, expected, in some cases detested, and the object of many a joke. This fun and whimsical recipe book of sweets will bring delight back into the fruitcake tradition! With these yummy new twists on timeless dessert recipes, we're hoping you're tempted to try a bite this year.

Many Christmas blessings!
MariLee Parrish

Fruits & Cakes

And she shall bring forth a son,
and thou shalt call his name Jesus:
for he shall save his people from their sins.

MATTHEW 1:21

Traditional Christmas Fruitcake

4 cups flour
1 teaspoon double-acting baking powder
½ teaspoon cloves
½ teaspoon cinnamon
¼ teaspoon mace
1 pound shortening
1 pound brown sugar
10 eggs, well beaten

½ pound each candied cherries and/or pineapple
1 pound each dates and raisins
½ pound candied orange and lemon peel
½ pound nuts, chopped
1 cup honey
1 cup light molasses
½ cup apple cider

Combine flour, baking powder, and spices. Sift together very well and set aside. Cream shortening. Gradually add sugar and cream until light and fluffy. Add eggs, fruits, nuts, honey, molasses, and cider. Add flour mixture gradually, beating well. Fold into three 5x10-inch loaf pans that have been greased, lined with parchment paper, and greased again. Bake at 250 degrees for 3½ to 4 hours. Allow to cool completely. Remove from pan and store in airtight container in a cool place for several weeks before serving. Can also be frozen after 1 or 2 weeks for up to 6 months.

A Yummy Fruitcake

Try this recipe if you're not a fan of traditional fruitcake!

⅓ cup unsalted butter (no substitutions)

3 tablespoons brown sugar

2 eggs, lightly beaten

3 tablespoons honey

½ cup flour

¼ teaspoon salt

½ teaspoon baking powder

⅛ teaspoon ground allspice

⅛ teaspoon freshly ground nutmeg

2 tablespoons half-and-half

1 cup cranberries (fresh or frozen)

1 cup chopped dates

6 ounces finely chopped dried apricots

2 cups pecans, halved or chopped

Cream butter, sugar, eggs, and honey. Combine dry ingredients and add to creamed butter mixture alternately with half-and-half. Beat in cranberries, dried fruit, and nuts. Fold into greased and floured loaf pans. Set one oven rack at lowest position and another oven rack at midlevel position and place shallow pan of boiling water on bottom rack. Bake fruitcake in center of midlevel rack at 300 degrees for 1 hour or until toothpick inserted in center comes out clean. Cool completely before removing from pan. Loosen edges with knife and place cake in airtight container. Refrigerate for at least 24 hours before serving. Best when refrigerated for several days.

Traditional fruitcakes should be made weeks or even months in advance. The cakes freeze well, but the traditional ingredients need time to age before freezing. If you've tried a fruitcake before and didn't care for the taste, it may be because it was not aged properly. Fruitcake ingredients need to mellow for at least three or four weeks before they taste the way they are meant to taste.

Super-Quick Pound Cake

1 box vanilla pudding pound cake mix

1 cup flour

1 cup sour cream

1 cup sweet milk

4 eggs

¾ cup sugar

½ teaspoon vanilla

½ teaspoon butter

½ teaspoon almond extract

½ teaspoon lemon extract

Preheat oven to 350 degrees. Combine all ingredients in large mixing bowl and beat for 2 minutes. Pour into greased pound cake baking pan. Bake for 1 hour and 10 minutes. Cool for 5 minutes in pan before serving.

Ice Water Chocolate Cake

¾ cup margarine

2¼ cups sugar

1½ teaspoons vanilla

3 eggs

3 (1 ounce) squares baking
   chocolate, melted

3 cups flour

1½ teaspoons baking soda

¾ teaspoon salt

1½ cups ice water

Blend margarine, sugar, and vanilla until mixture is consistency of
whipping cream. Add eggs, one at a time, then chocolate. Sift flour,
baking soda, and salt; add to creamy mixture alternately with ice water.
Spread in greased 9x13-inch pan and bake at 350 degrees for
45 minutes.

Time was with most of us, when Christmas Day, encircling all our limited world like a magic ring, left nothing out for us to miss or seek; bound together all our home enjoyments, affections, and hopes; grouped everything and everyone round the Christmas fire, and made the little picture shining in our bright young eyes complete.

CHARLES DICKENS

Chocolate Toffee Bar Cake

1 box German chocolate cake mix

1 (14 ounce) can sweetened condensed milk

1 jar caramel ice cream topping

8 ounces frozen whipped topping, thawed

3 to 6 milk chocolate toffee candy bars, crushed

Bake cake according to package directions. While cake is still hot, poke holes in cake about 1 inch apart, using handle of wooden spoon. Combine milk and caramel topping; pour evenly over cake. Refrigerate overnight. Before serving, top with whipped topping and sprinkle with crushed candy bars.

Fruitful Pizza

1 tube refrigerated cookie dough

1 (8 ounce) package cream
   cheese

⅓ cup sugar

½ teaspoon vanilla

Fresh fruit, cut into small pieces
   (bananas, apples, mandarin
   oranges, strawberries, peaches,
   pineapple, kiwi)

2 tablespoons orange marmalade

½ teaspoon water

Preheat oven to 375 degrees. Slice cookie dough and lay slices on pizza
pan. Flatten and spread slices to completely cover pan with dough.
Bake for 12 minutes. Let cool. In bowl, mix cream cheese, sugar, and
vanilla. Spread mixture onto cooled dough. Arrange fruit on top. Mix
orange marmalade with water and pour glaze over fruit. Chill and cut
into pizza slices.

Roman Apple Cake

4 cups chopped apples	2 cups flour
2 cups sugar	2 teaspoons cinnamon
½ cup vegetable oil	2 teaspoons baking soda
2 teaspoons vanilla	1 teaspoon salt
2 eggs	1 cup chopped nuts

Blend all ingredients until well moistened. Spread in greased 9x13-inch pan and bake at 350 degrees for 40 minutes.

Dump-It Cake

1 (20 ounce) can crushed
   pineapple, with juice
1 (21 ounce) can cherry pie filling

1 box yellow cake mix
½ cup chopped pecans (optional)
¾ cup butter, sliced

Spread pineapple with juice in 9x13-inch pan; layer cherry pie filling on top. Sprinkle yellow cake mix over pie filling layer—do not mix or stir. Scatter pecans on top. Dot with butter and bake at 350 degrees for 50 to 55 minutes.

Oatmeal Chocolate Chip Cake

1¾ cups boiling water

1 cup oats, quick or old-fashioned

1 cup brown sugar

1 cup sugar

½ cup margarine

2 eggs (3 if small)

1¾ cups flour

1 teaspoon baking soda

½ teaspoon salt

1 tablespoon cocoa

1 cup semisweet chocolate chips, divided

¾ cup chopped walnuts

Pour boiling water over oats; let stand at room temperature for 10 minutes. Add both sugars and margarine to oatmeal. Stir until margarine melts. Add eggs and mix well. Stir in flour, baking soda, salt, and cocoa. Stir in ½ cup chocolate chips. Pour into greased 9x13-inch pan. Sprinkle walnuts and remaining ½ cup chocolate chips on top. Bake at 350 degrees for 40 minutes. Needs no frosting.

Let us now go even unto Bethlehem,
and see this thing which is come to pass,
which the Lord hath made known unto us.

LUKE 2:15

Carrot Cake

1¾ cups flour

½ teaspoon baking soda

1 teaspoon cinnamon

¼ teaspoon salt

1½ cups sugar

½ teaspoon nutmeg

3 eggs

1 cup vegetable oil

1 cup shredded carrots

1 cup finely chopped pecans

Sift all dry ingredients. Add eggs and oil; mix well. Add carrots and pecans; stir until well mixed. Bake at 350 degrees for 55 minutes. Best topped with cream cheese frosting.

Chocolate Zucchini Cake

1 cup brown sugar

½ cup sugar

½ cup margarine

½ cup vegetable oil

3 eggs

1 teaspoon vanilla

½ cup buttermilk

2½ cups flour

½ teaspoon allspice

½ teaspoon cinnamon

½ teaspoon salt

2 teaspoons baking soda

¼ cup cocoa

1¾ cups shredded zucchini, drained

1 cup semisweet chocolate chips

Cream brown sugar, sugar, margarine, and vegetable oil. Add eggs, vanilla, buttermilk, and flour; stir well. Sift allspice, cinnamon, salt, baking soda, and cocoa. Add to creamed mixture and beat well. Stir in zucchini and pour into 9x13-inch pan. Sprinkle chocolate chips on top. Bake at 325 degrees for 45 minutes.

Pumpkin Cake Loaf

1¼ cups sugar
½ cup butter
2 eggs, beaten
2 cups flour, sifted
3 teaspoons baking powder
½ teaspoon salt
½ teaspoon cinnamon
½ teaspoon ginger

½ teaspoon nutmeg
1 cup canned pumpkin
¾ cup milk
1 teaspoon vanilla
¾ teaspoon baking soda
1 cup mini chocolate chips
Powdered sugar

Cream together sugar and butter. Blend in eggs. Sift together flour, baking powder, salt, and spices. Mix pumpkin, milk, vanilla, and baking soda together. Add flour to milk mixture alternately with sugar and egg mixture. Stir in chocolate chips. Bake at 325 degrees in greased loaf pan for 45 minutes or until toothpick inserted in center of cake comes out clean. Run knife around outer edge of cake after 5 minutes of cooling and remove from pan; cool on wire rack. Dust with powdered sugar.

Cinnamon Brownie Cake

1 cup butter

1 cup water

2 eggs

½ cup milk

2 cups flour

2 cups sugar

2 heaping teaspoons cinnamon

1 heaping teaspoon baking soda

4 tablespoons cocoa

1 teaspoon vanilla

Frosting:

½ cup butter

6 tablespoons milk

1 pound powdered sugar

4 tablespoons cocoa

1 cup chopped pecans

1 teaspoon vanilla

Preheat oven to 400 degrees. Bring butter and water to a boil in small saucepan. In small bowl, beat eggs and milk. In large bowl, combine dry ingredients. Stir egg mixture into dry ingredients and mix well. Slowly stir in hot butter and water mixture a little at a time so as not to cook eggs. Add vanilla and pour into greased jelly roll pan. Bake for 20 minutes or until brownies test done. Frosting: Bring butter and milk to a boil. Stir in remaining ingredients. Spread over warm cake.

Lemon Cake Bars

1 (18 ounce) box lemon cake mix
  with pudding
1 egg
½ cup vegetable oil

1 (8 ounce) package cream cheese
¼ cup sugar
1 tablespoon lemon juice

Combine cake mix, egg, and oil. Mix well. Reserve 1 cup mixture for topping and press the rest into ungreased 9x13-inch pan with fork. Bake at 350 degrees for 15 minutes. Cool. In medium bowl, beat cream cheese, sugar, and lemon juice until smooth. Spread evenly over crust. Crumble reserved cake mix over top. Bake for 15 minutes or until filling is set. Cool and serve.

Mississippi Mud Cake

3 tablespoons cocoa
2 cups sugar
1 cup butter
1 teaspoon vanilla
4 eggs
1½ cups flour
1⅓ cups flaked coconut
1 cup chopped pecans
1 large jar marshmallow creme

Frosting:
½ cup cocoa
½ cup evaporated milk
1 teaspoon vanilla
1 pound powdered sugar
½ cup butter
½ cup chopped pecans

Preheat oven to 350 degrees. In large bowl, cream cocoa, sugar, and butter. Add vanilla and eggs and mix well. Add flour, coconut, and 1 cup pecans. Beat for 2 minutes. Bake in greased 9x13-inch baking pan for 35 to 40 minutes. While cake is still hot, gently spread marshmallow creme over top and let cool. Frosting: In bowl, beat together cocoa, evaporated milk, vanilla, powdered sugar, and butter until smooth and spread over marshmallow creme. Sprinkle chopped pecans over top.

Easy Mini Cheesecakes

1 dozen vanilla wafers
2 (8 ounce) packages cream
  cheese

1 teaspoon vanilla
½ cup sugar
2 eggs

Line muffin pan with 12 foil liners. Place vanilla wafer in each liner. In mixing bowl, combine cream cheese, vanilla, and sugar. Beat well. Add eggs and beat until well blended. Pour cream cheese mixture over wafers. Fill each liner about three quarters full. Bake at 325 degrees for 25 minutes. Garnish with fruit or chocolate.

Need frosting but don't have the time to make any? Sprinkle a bag of milk chocolate chips on top while the cake or brownies are still warm. Let them sit for a few minutes. The chips will melt and then you can spread as you would icing.

Apple-Cranberry Dump Cake

1 (16 ounce) can whole cranberry
  sauce
1 (21 ounce) can apple pie filling
1 box yellow cake mix

1 stick butter
½ cup chopped pecans
Whipped topping

Dump cranberries into ungreased 9x13-inch baking pan. Dump apple pie filling into pan. Spread mixture evenly and sprinkle dry cake mix on top. Cut up butter and dot top of cake. Sprinkle pecans over all. Bake at 325 degrees for 65 minutes or until wooden pick inserted in center comes out clean. Let cool. Top with whipped topping and serve.

Strawberry Trifle

1 angel food cake, cubed

1 small box vanilla instant pudding

1 cup cold milk

1 pint vanilla ice cream, slightly thawed

1 small box strawberry gelatin

1 cup boiling water

1 (10 ounce) package frozen strawberries, slightly thawed

In 9x9-inch glass baking dish, place cubed angel food cake. In separate bowl, combine pudding mix, milk, and ice cream; beat until smooth and pour over cake. Dissolve gelatin in boiling water. Add strawberries and cool slightly; spoon over pudding layer. Cover and refrigerate overnight.

Cake in a Mug

4 tablespoons flour

4 tablespoons sugar

2 tablespoons cocoa

1 egg

3 tablespoons milk

3 tablespoons vegetable oil

3 tablespoons mini chocolate chips

⅛ teaspoon vanilla

Whipped cream

Add dry ingredients to large microwavable mug and mix well. Add egg and mix thoroughly. Add milk and oil. Mix well. Add chocolate chips and vanilla, and mix again. Microwave for 3 minutes on high. Cake will rise over top of mug. Allow to cool a little, top with whipped cream, and serve.

Piña Colada Cake

1 box yellow cake mix

1 small can crushed pineapple

1 (14 ounce) can sweetened
   condensed milk

1 small can cream of coconut

Whipped topping

Flaked coconut

Make yellow cake according to directions on box. While still hot, poke
holes in cake and pour pineapple, sweetened condensed milk, and
cream of coconut over it. Let cake cool and top with whipped topping.
Garnish with flaked coconut.

May you have the gladness
of Christmas, which is hope.

AVA HENDRICKS

Strawberry Gelatin Cake

½ cup water

1 (3 ounce) package strawberry gelatin

1 box white cake mix

1 cup vegetable oil

4 eggs

3 tablespoons flour

1 cup strawberries (fresh or frozen)

Frosting:

½ cup butter, softened

1 pound powdered sugar

⅓ cup strawberries

Preheat oven to 350 degrees. Bring water to a boil. Stir in gelatin and set aside. In separate bowl, combine cake mix and oil. Mix until smooth. Add eggs and flour. Mix until smooth again. Add gelatin and strawberries. Pour into greased 9x13-inch baking pan. Bake gelatin for 35 minutes or until cake tests done.

Frosting: Blend softened butter, powdered sugar, and strawberries until smooth. Frost cooled cake.

Biscuit Coffee Cake

2 tubes refrigerated buttermilk biscuits

⅓ cup firmly packed brown sugar

¼ cup butter, melted

1 teaspoon cinnamon

⅓ cup pecans

Preheat oven to 350 degrees. In lightly greased 9x9-inch pan, arrange biscuits, overlapping edges. Combine remaining ingredients and spread evenly over biscuits. Bake for 15 minutes or until done.

Wacky Cake

3 cups flour

2 cups sugar

½ cup cocoa

2 teaspoons baking soda

1 teaspoon salt

⅔ cup vegetable oil

2 teaspoons vanilla

2 tablespoons vinegar

2 cups warm water

Sift flour, sugar, cocoa, baking soda, and salt in large bowl. Make three wells in dry mixture. Pour oil and vanilla in one well, vinegar in another, and water in the third. Mix well. Pour into greased 9x13-inch pan that has been dusted with cocoa. Bake at 350 degrees for 35 minutes.

Jan's Blackberry-Pineapple Delight

1 can blackberry pie filling

1 can crushed pineapple

1 box yellow cake mix

1 stick butter

Finely chopped pecans

Mix pie filling and pineapple. Pour into ungreased 9x13-inch pan. Sprinkle cake mix over top. Cut butter into thin slices and place on top of cake mix; sprinkle with pecans as desired. Bake at 350 degrees for 45 minutes. Refrigerate when cool.

Raspberry Fruit Pizza

1 (20 ounce) package refrigerated sugar cookie dough

1 (8 ounce) package cream cheese, softened

⅓ cup sugar

½ teaspoon vanilla

Assorted fresh fruit, sliced

½ cup raspberry preserves

2 tablespoons cold water

Press cookie dough into round or rectangular pizza pan. Bake at 375 degrees for 12 minutes or until golden brown. Cool. Meanwhile, beat cream cheese, sugar, and vanilla until smooth. Spread over crust. Arrange fruit over cream cheese layer. Mix preserves and water and spoon over fruit. Refrigerate. Cut into wedges.

Whipped Cream Cake

1½ cups butter
3 cups sugar
6 eggs

3 cups flour
½ pint whipping cream

Cream butter and sugar. Add eggs, one at a time, beating after each addition. Beginning and ending with flour, alternately add flour and cream. (Do not whip cream.) Lightly grease and flour tube pan. Pour mixture into pan and bake at 300 degrees for 2 hours.

It is Christmas in the heart that
puts Christmas in the air.

W. T. ELLIS

Easy Cake Mix Apple Crisp

6 apples, peeled and sliced

1 cup water

1 box white cake mix

1 cup brown sugar

½ cup margarine, melted

1 teaspoon cinnamon

Vanilla ice cream

Arrange apples in bottom of ungreased 9x13-inch pan; top with water. In separate bowl, combine cake mix, brown sugar, margarine, and cinnamon; stir until blended (mixture will be crumbly). Sprinkle crumb mixture over apple slices. Bake at 350 degrees for 50 minutes or until lightly browned and bubbly. Serve warm with vanilla ice cream.

Punch Bowl Layer Cake

2 small boxes vanilla instant
  pudding mix

3⅓ cups milk

12 ounces frozen whipped topping,
  thawed, divided

1 box vanilla wafers

1 large can crushed pineapple,
  drained

3 bananas, sliced

Mix pudding with milk and half of whipped topping. Place one layer
of wafers in punch bowl or clear glass serving bowl; top with half of
pineapple, half of bananas, and half of pudding mixture; repeat. Top
with remaining whipped topping. Refrigerate until ready to serve.

Mary's Pumpkin Pie Cake

1 (29 ounce) can pumpkin
1 (12 ounce) can evaporated milk
3 eggs
1 cup sugar
½ teaspoon salt

4 teaspoons pumpkin pie spice
1 box spice (or carrot) cake mix
¾ cup butter
1 cup chopped pecans

Lightly grease 9x13-inch baking pan. Combine pumpkin, evaporated milk, eggs, sugar, salt, and pumpkin pie spice. Mix well. Pour batter into prepared pan. Sprinkle dry cake mix evenly over pumpkin mixture. Melt butter and drizzle over cake mix. Sprinkle pecans over top. Bake at 350 degrees for 55 minutes or until done.

To keep brown sugar from hardening, just store it in the freezer! When you need it, pull it out of the freezer 20 minutes before use. You can also add ½ piece of bread to your brown sugar if you prefer to keep the brown sugar at room temperature.

Leah's Pumpkin Cranberry Bread

½ cup orange juice

1 cup dried cranberries

3 cups sugar

4 large eggs

1 (15 ounce) can pumpkin

1 cup vegetable oil

3 cups flour

2 teaspoons cinnamon

1 teaspoon ginger

½ teaspoon cloves

2 teaspoons baking soda

1 teaspoon salt

Preheat oven to 350 degrees. In small bowl, mix orange juice and cranberries; set aside. In another bowl, cream sugar and eggs; add pumpkin and oil. Add flour, cinnamon, ginger, cloves, baking soda, and salt. Mix thoroughly. Pour in orange juice and cranberries; stir by hand. Pour into 2 loaf pans and bake for 60 minutes.

Nuts & Bolts

For unto us a child is born, unto us a son is given: and the government shall be upon his shoulder: and his name shall be called Wonderful, Counsellor, The mighty God, The everlasting Father, The Prince of Peace.

<small>ISAIAH 9:6</small>

Mama's Old-Fashioned Nuts and Bolts

2 cups corn squares cereal

2 cups rice squares cereal

2 cups croutons

2 cups thin pretzels

1 cup cashews

1 cup peanuts

⅔ cup butter

1 tablespoon seasoning salt

1 teaspoon marjoram

1 teaspoon garlic powder

1 teaspoon summer savory (or similar)

1 teaspoon onion powder

Dash or two of Worcestershire sauce

Place cereals, croutons, pretzels, and nuts in large baking pans. Melt butter in saucepan and add all spices. Spoon evenly over cereal mixture in pans. Bake at 250 degrees for 45 minutes. Stir every 10 minutes. Store in cool place.

White Chocolate Cranberry Snack Mix

4 cups oatmeal squares cereal
1½ cups uncooked oats
1 cup chopped unsalted pecans
1 teaspoon cinnamon
¼ teaspoon sea salt

½ cup butter
½ cup light brown sugar
½ cup honey
1 cup sweetened dried cranberries
1 cup white chocolate chips

Line two 9x13-inch pans with aluminum foil. Spray foil with nonstick spray. Set aside. Mix together oatmeal squares, oats, pecans, cinnamon, and salt in very large bowl. Set aside. In saucepan, melt butter and stir in brown sugar and honey. Stir over low heat until sugar has dissolved. Pour melted butter mixture in a thin stream over cereal mixture while stirring with a large spoon. Spread mixture evenly in a single layer in foil-lined pan. Bake at 325 degrees for 10 minutes. Stir. Bake for another 10 minutes. Add cranberries and stir. Bake for another 10 minutes. Spread evenly over wax paper to cool. Melt white chocolate chips in microwave for 30 seconds at a time until melted. Drizzle over snack mix. Allow to cool completely before storing snack mix in airtight container.

Good news from heaven the angels bring,

Glad tidings to the earth they sing:

To us this day a child is given,

To crown us with the joy of heaven.

MARTIN LUTHER

Nana's Texas Tumbleweeds

1 pound almond bark

1 (12 ounce) package peanut
butter chips

1 (12.5 ounce) can salted peanuts

2 (1⅝ ounce) cans potato sticks

Combine almond bark and peanut butter chips in large pot and stir
over medium-low heat until melted. Stir in peanuts and potato sticks.
Drop by teaspoons onto wax paper–lined cookie sheets. Chill until set.
Makes about 4 dozen.

Daddy's Puppy Chow

Melt together: 1 cup chunky peanut butter
1 cup milk chocolate chips   ½ cup butter

In a separate large bowl that has a fitted lid, mix together:
8 cups Chex cereal

1 cup peanuts

Add chocolate chip/peanut butter/butter mixture. Then add 2½ cups
powdered sugar. Place lid on bowl and shake.

Leah's Krispy Caramel Balls

1 can sweetened condensed milk
1 bag caramels, unwrapped
½ cup margarine
1 teaspoon vanilla

Pinch salt
½ box crisp rice cereal
1 bag large marshmallows

In double boiler stir milk, caramels, margarine, vanilla, and salt until melted. Turn down heat to medium. In separate bowl, pour ½ box of cereal and crush slightly with hands. Dip marshmallows in caramel sauce, then roll in cereal to coat. Place on wax paper to cool.

Peacock Pottery's
Cinnamon-Candied Popcorn

8 quarts plain popped popcorn

1 cup butter

½ cup light corn syrup

1 (8 ounce) package cinnamon red hot candies

Preheat oven to 250 degrees. Place popped popcorn in large mixing bowl and set aside. In saucepan, combine butter, corn syrup, and red hot candies. Cook over medium heat, stirring constantly, until boiling. Boil for 5 minutes, stirring occasionally. Pour over popcorn and mix thoroughly. Divide between 2 lightly greased cake pans. Bake for 1 hour, stirring every 15 minutes. Remove from oven and place on wax paper to cool. Break into pieces and store in airtight container.

Leah's Chocolate-Covered Macadamia Nuts

1 cup semisweet chocolate chips   ¾ cup peanut butter chips
½ cup butterscotch chips   5 to 6 cups macadamia nuts

Put all chips in mixing bowl; microwave in 15-second increments, stirring after each time until all chips are melted. Pour in macadamia nuts; stir until covered. Drop by spoonfuls onto wax paper and let stand until dry. Can be kept in the freezer, too.

Munch Mix

1 (9 ounce) bag sweet and salty
    snack mix with cereal and
    pretzels

1 (6 ounce) package corn snack
    (such as Bugles)

1 (6 ounce) box cheese crackers

1 cup peanuts or mixed nuts
    (optional)

1 cup candy-coated chocolate
    pieces (optional)

Combine all ingredients in large bowl.

Johnny Cake Corn Bread

¾ cup flour

teaspoon baking soda

2 tablespoons sugar

½ teaspoon salt

1¼ cups cornmeal

2 eggs

¼ cup vinegar

¼ cup butter, melted

Preheat oven to 400 degrees. In large bowl, sift together flour, baking soda, sugar, and salt; stir in cornmeal. In separate bowl, whisk together eggs, vinegar, and butter. Add to dry ingredients and mix until moist. Grease 9x9-inch baking dish. Pour in batter and bake for 30 minutes or until light brown.

Peanut Clusters

½ pound milk chocolate   1 cup unsalted peanuts
⅔ cup sweetened condensed milk

Use double boiler to melt chocolate. Remove from heat and stir in
sweetened condensed milk. Add peanuts and mix until peanuts are
well covered. Drop by spoonfuls onto greased cookie sheet. Refrigerate
for 3 hours before serving.

What is Christmas? It is a fervent
wish that every cup may overflow
with blessings rich and eternal,
and that every path may lead to peace.

AGNES M. PHARO

Dump Cake

1 cup butter

1 large can crushed pineapple, with juice

1 (15 ounce) can cherry pie filling

1 box yellow cake mix

2 cups chopped nuts

Whipped cream

Preheat oven to 325 degrees. In small saucepan, melt butter and pour into 9x13-inch baking pan. Dump pineapple with juice into baking pan, then pie filling, then cake mix, and finally nuts, spreading out each layer evenly. Bake for 1 hour or until cherry pie filling oozes through other ingredients and nuts are brown. Serve with whipped cream.

Gramps's Microwave Peanut Brittle

1 cup sugar

½ cup light corn syrup

1 cup raw peanuts

⅛ teaspoon salt

1 tablespoon butter

1 teaspoon vanilla

1 teaspoon baking soda

Combine sugar, corn syrup, peanuts, and salt in 2-quart microwavable mixing bowl. Microwave on high for 8 minutes, stirring after 4 minutes. Add butter. Microwave on high for 2 minutes. Brittle should not get too brown. Stir in vanilla and baking soda until light and foamy. Spread on buttered baking sheet as thinly as possible. Cool. Break into pieces.

Chocolate Crunch Cupcakes

4 (1 ounce) squares semisweet
   baking chocolate

1 teaspoon vanilla

1 cup chopped nuts of choice

4 large eggs, beaten

1 cup butter

1 cup flour

1¾ cups sugar

Preheat oven to 325 degrees. Melt chocolate in saucepan. Add vanilla and nuts. In bowl, mix together beaten eggs, butter, flour, and sugar. Carefully add to chocolate mixture. Pour into paper liners set in muffin pans and bake for 35 minutes.

If your cake or bread recipe calls for nuts, heat them first in the oven, then dust with powdered sugar before adding to the batter to add a bit more sweetness and to keep them from settling to the bottom of the pan.

Blueberry Bread

2 cups flour
1 cup sugar
1½ teaspoons baking powder
½ teaspoon baking soda
¼ teaspoon salt
2 tablespoons shortening

1 egg
Boiling water
¼ cup orange juice
1 tablespoon orange zest
1 cup blueberries
½ cup chopped walnuts

Preheat oven to 350 degrees. Grease 5x9-inch loaf pan. In large bowl, mix flour, sugar, baking powder, baking soda, and salt thoroughly. Cut in shortening. Stir in egg. Add enough boiling water to orange juice and zest to measure 1 cup. Stir into flour mixture. Fold in blueberries and nuts. Pour batter into prepared pan. Bake for 60 minutes.

Puffed Corn

½ pound butter (no substitutions)   ½ cup light corn syrup

1 cup brown sugar   2 bags microwave popcorn, popped

Preheat oven to 275 degrees. In saucepan, bring butter, brown sugar, and corn syrup to a boil and let boil for 3 minutes. Put popcorn in large bowl. Pour sugar mixture over popcorn and mix to coat well. Spread on cookie sheets and bake for 45 minutes, stirring every 10 minutes. Break apart when cool and store in airtight containers.

Homemade Granola

8 cups whole oats
1½ cups bran
1½ cups wheat germ
1 cup flaked coconut
¾ cup brown sugar

1 cup pecans
¾ cup canola oil
1 cup honey
2 teaspoons vanilla

Preheat oven to 325 degrees. In large bowl, mix oats, bran, wheat germ, coconut, brown sugar, and pecans. Heat canola oil, honey, and vanilla in small saucepan to boiling. Pour over oat mixture. Mix well and spread in 2 greased 9x13-inch baking pans. Bake until golden brown, 25 to 30 minutes. Check and stir every 10 minutes. Remove from oven, pour onto trays, and cool for 2 hours. Store in airtight Christmas containers and give as festive gifts.

Date Bread

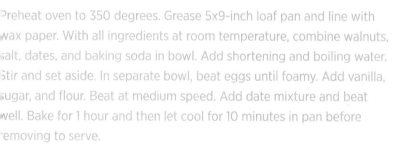

1 cup chopped walnuts	¼ cup boiling water
½ teaspoon salt	2 eggs
1 cup pitted, chopped dates	1 teaspoon vanilla
1½ teaspoons baking soda	1 cup sugar
¼ cup shortening	1½ cups sifted flour

Preheat oven to 350 degrees. Grease 5x9-inch loaf pan and line with wax paper. With all ingredients at room temperature, combine walnuts, salt, dates, and baking soda in bowl. Add shortening and boiling water. Stir and set aside. In separate bowl, beat eggs until foamy. Add vanilla, sugar, and flour. Beat at medium speed. Add date mixture and beat well. Bake for 1 hour and then let cool for 10 minutes in pan before removing to serve.

O little town of Bethlehem
How still we see thee lie
Above thy deep and dreamless sleep
The silent stars go by
Yet in thy dark streets shineth
The everlasting Light
The hopes and fears of all the years
Are met in thee tonight

PHILLIPS BROOKS

Quick 'n' Easy Fudge

2 (8 ounce) boxes semisweet
chocolate squares

1 (14 ounce) can sweetened
condensed milk

1 cup chopped walnuts

2 teaspoons vanilla

Place chocolate and milk in microwave-safe bowl. Microwave on high
until chocolate melts, stirring often. Add walnuts and vanilla; stir. Pour
into buttered 9x9-inch pan. Refrigerate before serving.

69

Nutty Monkey Bread

2½ cups sugar, divided
1 tablespoon cinnamon
3 tubes refrigerated biscuits

1 tablespoon vanilla
1 cup margarine
Chopped nuts

Preheat oven to 350 degrees. In bowl, mix together 1 cup sugar and cinnamon. Quarter biscuits and roll them in sugar mixture. Place in 9x13-inch baking pan. Sprinkle remaining cinnamon/sugar mixture over biscuits. Set aside. Melt together vanilla, 1½ cups sugar, and margarine and pour over biscuits. Bake 30 minutes. Top with chopped nuts.

Festive Lemon-Lime Soda Salad

1 package lemon gelatin

1 cup boiling water

1 (8 ounce) package cream cheese, softened

1 teaspoon sugar

1 teaspoon vanilla

3 drops green food coloring

1 cup canned pineapple, drained

10 ounces lemon-lime soda

½ cup chopped nuts

Dissolve gelatin in boiling water. Add cream cheese and beat. Fold in sugar, vanilla, and green food coloring. Add drained pineapple, lemon-lime soda, and nuts. Stir after mixture thickens to keep nuts from floating to the top.

Honey Peanut Butter Cereal Bars

1 cup peanut butter

⅔ cup honey

4 cups crispy rice cereal

2 cups fruit/nut cereal of choice

In saucepan over medium heat, melt peanut butter and honey until creamy. Stir in cereals until well mixed. Spread onto wax paper and let cool before cutting into bars.

Gail's 10-Minute Toffee Treats

1 sleeve saltine crackers

1 cup butter

1 cup brown sugar

2 cups chocolate chips

½ cup chopped nuts and/or toffee bits

Preheat oven to 400 degrees. Line cookie sheet with foil; place single layer of saltines on foil. In saucepan, bring butter and brown sugar to a boil. Boil for 3 minutes. Immediately pour over saltines. Spread. Bake for only 4 to 5 minutes. Remove from oven and sprinkle chocolate chips over top. Wait 4 minutes and spread. Sprinkle with nuts/toffee. Cool and break into pieces.

I truly believe that if we keep telling the Christmas story, singing the Christmas songs, and living the Christmas spirit, we can bring joy and happiness and peace to this world.

NORMAN VINCENT PEALE

Gail's Chips, Cinnamon, 'n' Nuts Biscotti

¾ cup butter

1 cup sugar

2 eggs

1½ teaspoons vanilla

2½ cups flour

1 teaspoon cinnamon

¾ teaspoon baking powder

½ teaspoon salt

1 cup nuts of choice

½ to 1 cup chocolate or cinnamon chips (optional)

Preheat oven to 350 degrees. Grease cookie sheet. In medium bowl, cream together butter and sugar until light and fluffy. Beat in eggs and vanilla. Sift together flour, cinnamon, baking powder, and salt; mix into butter mixture. Stir in nuts/chips. Shape dough into 2 equal-sized "logs" approximately 12 inches long. Place logs on baking sheet and flatten to about ½ inch thickness. Bake for about 30 minutes or until center is firm. Once cool enough to handle, use serrated knife to slice logs diagonally into ½-inch-thick slices. Place slices on one side and bake for 10 more minutes, turning over after 5 minutes. Cool completely and store in airtight container.

Gotta Share It or You Will Eat It All Salted Caramel Pretzel Bark

½ bag mini pretzel twists
2 sticks butter
1 cup brown sugar

1 (12 ounce) package chocolate chips
Sea salt or table salt

Preheat oven to 350 degrees. Line large jelly roll pan with aluminum foil and lay single layer of pretzels down. In medium saucepan, melt butter and brown sugar until sugar is dissolved. Let boil gently just until mixture starts to stick to bottom and forms a nice smooth caramel. It needs to bubble a little and get pretty thick. Remove from heat and pour evenly over pretzels. Bake for 5 minutes. Remove from oven and sprinkle chocolate chips over top. Place back in oven for 1 minute to melt chips. Take out of oven and spread chips over caramel. Sprinkle with salt. Let cool for a few minutes and then pop into freezer for 2 to 3 hours. Once frozen, break into chunks.

Cookies & Cream

Faith is the root of all blessings.

JEREMY TAYLOR

Sara's Raspberry Butter Cookies

2 sticks butter, softened
3 heaping tablespoons sugar
2 teaspoons almond extract
2¾ cups sifted flour

Raspberry jam
Pecans
Powdered sugar

Cream butter and sugar until light and fluffy. Add almond extract and flour; mix. Roll dough into balls about 1 inch round. Arrange on cookie sheet. Make dent in each ball and fill with jam. Place pecan half on top. Bake at 350 degrees for 15 to 20 minutes. Remove and cool. Roll in powdered sugar.

Strawberry Cream Cheese Crescents

1 (8 ounce) tube refrigerated
   crescent rolls

Cream cheese
Strawberry preserves

Unroll crescent rolls and fill each with 1 tablespoon cream cheese and 1 to 2 teaspoons strawberry preserves. Roll. Bake according to package directions.

Aunt Brandy's Chocolate No-Bake Cookies

2 cups sugar
½ cup milk
1 stick butter

5 tablespoons cocoa
3 cups quick oats

In large pan, mix together sugar, milk, butter, and cocoa. Bring to a boil for 3 minutes. Add oats and remove from heat. Drop by spoonfuls onto wax paper and let set.

Chocolate Truffles

⅔ cup heavy whipping cream

2 cups semisweet or milk
   chocolate chips

2 teaspoons vanilla

In saucepan, heat cream almost to a boil. Remove from heat and add chocolate chips. Whisk gently until chocolate is melted and mixture is smooth. Stir in vanilla and pour into bowl. Cover and refrigerate for 3 hours or until firm. When chocolate mixture is solid enough to work with, scoop into 1-inch balls and roll in your favorite coatings, such as crushed cookies, sprinkles, powdered sugar, flaked coconut, chopped nuts, or colored sugars. Cover and refrigerate for 2 hours. Serve cold. Keep refrigerated in airtight container.

Somehow, not only for Christmas,
But all the long year through,
The joy that you give to others
Is the joy that comes back to you.

JOHN GREENLEAF WHITTIER

Strawberry Cream Cheese Crepes

⅔ cup milk

2 eggs

2 tablespoons sugar

6 tablespoons flour

2 tablespoons butter

Strawberry preserves

Cream cheese

In blender, mix all ingredients except butter, preserves, and cream cheese. Heat butter in small frying pan. Pour one-fourth of batter into pan. Flip when edges are brown. Recipe makes 4 crepes. Fill each crepe with 1 teaspoon preserves and 2 teaspoons cream cheese. Roll and serve.

Lemon Cream Cheese Bars

1 box lemon cake mix
½ cup butter
3 eggs, divided

1 (8 ounce) package cream cheese
1 (3 ounce) package lemon instant
  pudding mix

Preheat oven to 350 degrees. In bowl, combine cake mix, butter, and 1 egg and stir until moist. Press mixture into greased 9x13-inch baking dish. In separate bowl, mix cream cheese and pudding mix until smooth. Set aside ½ cup of this mixture for topping. To remaining cream cheese mixture, add 2 eggs and beat for 4 minutes. Spread onto cake mixture and bake for 35 minutes. Let cool and then spread the ½ cup reserved frosting mixture over top.

Confetti Cookies

1 cup butter

1 cup packed brown sugar

1 cup sugar

2 eggs

2 teaspoons vanilla

2¼ cups flour

1 teaspoon baking soda

1 cup multicolored candy-coated chocolate pieces

Preheat oven to 375 degrees. In large bowl, stir all ingredients together and drop onto ungreased baking sheet. Bake for 10 minutes. Let cool.

Leah's Ice Cream Roll

4 eggs, separated
¾ cup sugar, divided
½ cup cake flour
⅓ cup baking cocoa
1 teaspoon baking powder
Pinch salt

½ cup raspberry jam (I use homemade)
2 cups softened ice cream (vanilla, chocolate chip, chocolate)
Powdered sugar
Hot fudge sauce
Whipped cream

In bowl, beat egg whites until soft peaks form; gradually add ¼ cup sugar and beat until stiff peaks form. In another bowl, beat egg yolks and remaining sugar until thick—about 5 minutes. Add flour, cocoa, baking powder, and salt to yolk mixture and beat well. By hand, fold in egg white mixture. Line 10x15-inch jelly roll pan with wax paper and grease paper with cooking spray. Spread batter evenly in pan. Bake for 10 to 12 minutes at 375 degrees. Cool for 5 minutes. Invert cake onto kitchen towel (flour sack towels work best) dusted with powdered sugar. Gently peel off waxed paper. Roll up cake in towel, jelly roll-style, starting with short side. Set aside to cool.

When cool, unroll cake and spread jam to within ½ inch of edge. Top with softened ice cream. Roll up without towel. Place seam side down on platter. Cover and freeze—overnight is best. Take out of freezer, cut into slices, dust with powdered sugar, and then drizzle with hot fudge sauce and whipped cream.

Grandma Kuess's Anise Cookies

Plan ahead. These need to set overnight
or about 10 hours before baking!

3 eggs
1 cup sugar
1½ cups to 2 cups flour

½ teaspoon baking powder
1½ to 2 teaspoons anise extract

Beat eggs lightly; add sugar and continue beating for 3 minutes. Add flour, sifted with baking powder, and anise extract. Beat mixture for 5 more minutes. Drop onto sheets of aluminum foil (sized for a cookie sheet) sprayed with cooking spray about 1 inch apart. Let sheets stand overnight or 10 hours at room temperature. Bake at 350 for 10 to 15 minutes.

In a Hurry No-Bake Cookies

2½ cups sugar

½ cup milk

½ cup butter

½ cup peanut butter

3 cups quick oats

6 tablespoons cocoa

1 teaspoon vanilla

In medium saucepan over medium-high heat, mix sugar, milk, and butter. Bring to a boil and boil for 1 minute. In large mixing bowl, combine peanut butter, oats, cocoa, and vanilla. Add heated mixture to mixing bowl and mix well. Drop by rounded tablespoons onto wax paper. Allow time for cookies to set. Serve!

Mandarin Orange Pie

1 cup whipped cream

2 cups orange-flavored yogurt

½ cup canned mandarin orange slices, drained

1 graham cracker pie shell

Fold whipped cream into yogurt in large bowl. Stir in oranges. Pour into pie shell. Cover with plastic wrap. Let chill for at least 3 hours in refrigerator before serving. You can also freeze this pie and thaw slightly before serving.

Double Chocolate Cookies

½ cup butter, softened
3 ounces cream cheese, softened
1 egg

1 (18 ounce) box devil's food cake mix
1½ cups semisweet chocolate chips, divided

Beat together butter, cream cheese, and egg. Add cake mix and mix well. Stir in 1 cup chocolate chips. Roll dough into balls and place on ungreased cookie sheet. Press down on each ball with a glass to flatten. Bake at 375 degrees for 7 to 9 minutes. Cool for 2 minutes, then remove from cookie sheets to cool completely. Melt remaining chocolate chips and drizzle over cooled cookies.

Just about any cake mix will make a yummy cookie! Experiment with the following recipes by substituting your favorite cake mix with your favorite additions (nuts, chocolate chips, raisins, etc.).

Easy Cake Mix Cookies

1 box cake mix (any flavor)
1 large egg
¼ cup vegetable oil
¼ cup water

1 cup any of the following:
chopped nuts, raisins, quick
oats, flaked coconut, chocolate
chips, candy-coated chocolate
pieces

Preheat oven to 350 degrees. Combine cake mix, egg, oil, and water.
Beat until well blended. Stir in remaining ingredient(s). Drop by
teaspoonfuls about 1 inch apart onto greased cookie sheet. Bake for 12
to 15 minutes or until done.

Chocolate Crinkles

1 box chocolate cake mix
1 large egg
¼ cup vegetable oil

¼ cup water
1 cup chocolate chips
2 cups powdered sugar

Preheat oven to 350 degrees. Combine cake mix, egg, oil, and water. Beat until well blended. Stir in chocolate chips. Roll into balls and dip in powdered sugar. Place about 1 inch apart on greased cookie sheet. Bake for 12 to 15 minutes. Sprinkle with additional powdered sugar.

Peanut Butter Chocolate Chip Cake Mix Cookies

2 eggs

⅓ cup water

¼ cup softened butter

1 cup peanut butter

1 box vanilla cake mix, divided

1 (12 ounce) package chocolate chips

Preheat oven to 375 degrees. Beat eggs, water, butter, peanut butter, and half the cake mix with electric mixer until light and fluffy. Stir in remaining cake mix and chocolate chips. Drop by rounded teaspoonfuls onto ungreased baking sheet. Bake for 10 to 12 minutes.

Oatmeal Kiss Freezer Cookies

1 cup butter, softened (no substitutions)
1 cup powdered sugar
⅛ teaspoon salt

1 teaspoon vanilla
1¼ cups flour
1 cup quick oats
Chocolate kiss candies

Cream together butter, powdered sugar, salt, and vanilla. Stir in flour and oats. Shape dough into 2 long rolls, each 1½ inches in diameter. Wrap in wax paper. Chill for at least 2 hours or freeze for up to 3 months.

When ready to bake:
Cut dough into ¼-inch slices and place on cookie sheet. Top each with chocolate kiss. Bake at 350 degrees for 10 to 12 minutes or until golden brown.

Chocolate Ice Cream Balls

3 cups chocolate ice cream

15 chocolate sandwich cookies, crushed

1½ cups semisweet chocolate chips, melted

½ cup milk chocolate chips, melted

Using ice cream scoop, scoop ice cream into six balls. Roll in crushed cookies. Place on cookie sheet lined with waxed paper and freeze for 2 hours or until firm. Place frozen ice cream balls on wire rack. Spoon melted chocolate over each ball. Freeze again until firm, at least 1 hour. Remove from freezer 10 minutes before serving.

Cherries in the Snow

½ cup butter

½ cup brown sugar

2 cups flour

1 cup chopped pecans

1 (8 ounce) package cream cheese

2 tablespoons vanilla

1 cup powdered sugar

1 (8 ounce) container whipped topping, thawed

1 (15 ounce) can cherry pie filling

Preheat oven to 350 degrees. Melt butter and mix in bowl with brown sugar, flour, and pecans. Pat mixture lightly into 9x13-inch baking pan. Bake for 20 minutes and let cool for 5 minutes. In bowl, combine cream cheese, vanilla, powdered sugar, and whipped topping. Spread over warm crust. Top with cherry pie filling and refrigerate. Serve chilled.

Frozen Pumpkin Dessert

1 (8 ounce) package cream cheese, softened

½ cup sugar

¼ cup brown sugar

1 (16 ounce) can pumpkin

1 teaspoon pumpkin pie spice

1 (8 ounce) container whipped topping, thawed, divided

Slivered almonds, chopped (optional)

Beat cream cheese and sugars until well blended. Add pumpkin and spice. Mix well. Reserve ½ cup whipped topping. Gently add remaining whipped topping. Pour into 9x9-inch baking pan. Freeze for 4 hours or until firm. Top with reserved whipped topping. Add chopped slivered almonds if desired.

Saucepan Cookies

½ cup skim milk

2 cups sugar

3 tablespoons cocoa

3 tablespoons crunchy peanut
butter

½ cup butter (no substitutions)

3 cups quick oats

1 teaspoon vanilla

Combine milk, sugar, cocoa, peanut butter, and butter. Stir and bring to a boil over medium heat. Let boil for 1½ minutes but do not stir. Remove from heat. Stir in oats and vanilla. Drop by teaspoonfuls onto wax paper. Cool.

Healthy Snack Cookies

1 banana

1 cup crunchy peanut butter

½ cup sugar

½ cup packed brown sugar

2 eggs

1 cup whole-wheat flour

1 cup white flour

1 teaspoon baking soda

1 cup quick oats

1 cup raisins or chocolate chips

Mix banana, peanut butter, and sugars until smooth. Mix in eggs. Add flours and baking soda and mix until just blended. Stir in oats and raisins or chocolate chips. Bake at 300 degrees for 10 to 15 minutes or until golden brown.

Soft Batch Cookies

1 cup sugar

1 cup brown sugar

½ cup butter, softened

2 eggs

3 cups flour

1½ teaspoons baking soda

1 teaspoon salt

2 cups semisweet chocolate chips

Mix all ingredients, stirring in chocolate chips last. If dough is too dry, add small amount of water. Roll into balls and place on cookie sheet. Bake at 350 degrees for 10 to 12 minutes.

Mom's Pumpkin Cookies

1 teaspoon vanilla

1 cup sugar

1 cup shortening

1 cup pumpkin

1 egg

1 teaspoon baking soda

1 teaspoon baking powder

½ teaspoon cinnamon

½ teaspoon salt

2 cups flour

1 cup chopped walnuts

In large bowl, mix vanilla, sugar, shortening, and pumpkin. Beat egg and add to mixture. In separate bowl, combine baking soda, baking powder, cinnamon, salt, flour, and walnuts. Add to pumpkin mixture; mix well. Shape into balls and place on cookie sheet. Bake at 350 degrees for 10 to 15 minutes.

Oatmeal Cookies

4 cups quick oats

2 cups light brown sugar

1 cup butter, melted

2 eggs, beaten

1 teaspoon salt

1 teaspoon vanilla

½ cup chopped walnuts

Combine all ingredients and refrigerate overnight. Drop by rounded teaspoons onto greased cookie sheet. Bake at 350 degrees for 10 minutes.

Striped-Cookie Dessert

2 cups buttermilk

16 ounces frozen whipped topping, thawed

2 small boxes vanilla instant pudding mix

2 small cans mandarin oranges, drained

1 package fudge-striped cookies, frozen and crushed

Combine all ingredients except cookies. Refrigerate until ready to serve. Stir in cookies just before serving.

Love is what's in the room
with you at Christmas if you
stop opening presents and listen.

UNKNOWN

Banana Pudding Pie

2 bananas, sliced

1 (9 inch) chocolate crumb piecrust

1 small box French vanilla instant pudding mix

8 ounces frozen whipped topping, thawed

Crushed chocolate sandwich cookies (optional)

Place sliced bananas in bottom of piecrust. Prepare pudding according to package directions. Pour pudding over bananas; allow to set. Top with whipped topping. Garnish with crushed chocolate sandwich cookies if desired. Refrigerate until ready to serve.

Gail's Kiss Surprise Cookies

½ cup shortening

¾ cup peanut butter

⅓ cup sugar (plus extra for rolling cookies in)

⅓ cup brown sugar

1 egg

2 tablespoons milk

1 teaspoon vanilla

1½ cups flour

1 teaspoon baking soda

½ teaspoon salt

48 chocolate kisses, unwrapped

Heat oven to 375 degrees. Beat shortening and peanut butter in large bowl until well blended. Add ⅓ cup sugar and brown sugar and beat until fluffy. Add egg, milk, and vanilla; beat well. Stir together flour, baking soda, and salt; gradually beat into peanut butter mixture. Shape dough into roughly 1-inch balls. Press chocolate kiss into each ball, hiding it in the middle of the ball. Roll balls in sugar and place on cookie sheets. Bake for 8 to 10 minutes. Cool completely on wire rack.

No-Roll Sugar Cookies

1 cup shortening

1 cup butter or margarine

3 cups sugar (plus extra for
  dipping glass into)

4 eggs

2 teaspoons vanilla

1 cup cornmeal

2½ teaspoons baking powder

1½ teaspoons butter-flavored salt

5½ cups flour

In 6-quart bowl, beat shortening and butter until creamy. Add sugar and beat until fluffy. Add eggs and vanilla and beat well. Mix together cornmeal, baking powder, and salt. Add to creamed mixture and blend well. Add flour gradually and mix well. Drop onto greased cookie sheets. Dip bottom of flat glass into sugar and press down on dough to flatten to ¼ inch. Bake at 350 degrees for 10 to 12 minutes.

Chocolate Delight

2 cups milk

1 small box chocolate instant pudding mix

2 cups frozen whipped topping, thawed, divided

Chocolate garnish (chocolate chips, grated chocolate, chocolate cookie crumbs) or strawberries

Using 2 cups milk, prepare pudding according to package directions. Fold 1½ cups whipped topping into pudding; spoon into 4 dessert dishes. Top with remaining ½ cup whipped topping and chocolate garnish or strawberries.

Peanut Butter Kiss Cookies

½ cup shortening
¾ cup peanut butter
⅓ cup sugar
⅓ cup brown sugar
1 egg
2 tablespoons milk

1 teaspoon vanilla
1½ cups flour
1 teaspoon baking soda
½ teaspoon salt
1 (8 ounce) package chocolate kisses, unwrapped

Preheat oven to 375 degrees. Beat shortening and peanut butter in large bowl until well blended. Add sugar and brown sugar and beat until fluffy. Add egg, milk, and vanilla; beat well. In separate bowl, combine flour, baking soda, and salt. Gradually beat into peanut butter mixture. Drop by tablespoonfuls onto ungreased cookie sheet. Bake for 8 to 10 minutes or until brown. Immediately press chocolate kiss into center of each cookie and transfer cookies to wire rack to cool completely.

Christmas Eve Cookies

1 cup sugar
½ cup butter
½ cup shortening
1 egg, separated

2 cups flour
½ teaspoon salt
1 tablespoon cinnamon
1 cup chopped pecans

Grease and flour 10x15-inch jelly roll pan. Cream sugar, butter, and shortening. Add egg yolk and dry ingredients (except pecans). Press into pan. Beat egg white until foamy and spread very thinly over batter. Press pecans on top. Bake at 350 degrees for about 30 minutes. Cut into squares and serve.

Dasher & Dancer

Bless us, Lord, this Christmas, with quietness of mind;
Teach us to be patient and always to be kind.

HELEN STEINER RICE

Reindeer Snacks

5 cups honeycomb-shaped cereal

2 cups small pretzel sticks, broken in half

½ cup butter

½ cup crunchy peanut butter

1 (12 ounce) package chocolate chips

1 cup powdered sugar

1 cup red and green candy-coated chocolate pieces

Combine cereal and pretzels in large bowl; set aside. Microwave butter, peanut butter, and chocolate chips on high for 45 seconds; stir. Continue microwaving until butter and chocolate are melted. Stir until smooth. Pour chocolate mixture over cereal in bowl; stir until coated. Spread mixture evenly into single layer on wax paper–lined baking sheets. Refrigerate for 20 minutes to set. Break into bite-sized pieces and place in large airtight container. And powdered sugar and chocolate candy pieces. Shake to mix well. To serve, spoon mixture into ice cream cones (for feeding reindeer, of course) if desired.

Reindeer Bark

2 (12 ounce) bags white chocolate chips

1½ cups crispy rice cereal

2 cups peanut butter crunch cereal

1½ cups peanuts

½ cup raisins

Melt white chocolate chips and mix with rest of ingredients. Spread on lightly buttered cookie sheet. Cool and break into small chunks.

Reindeer Crunch Balls

3 sticks butter (no substitutions)

3 to 4 cups powdered sugar

1 (16 ounce) jar crunchy peanut butter

2 (12 ounce) packages of semisweet chocolate chips

Melt butter over medium heat. Add powdered sugar and peanut butter. Mix well. Allow to cool enough to roll into small balls. Place balls on wax paper–lined trays and freeze for 1 hour. Melt chocolate in microwave 1 minute at a time until melted. Dip balls into chocolate. Place on wax paper and keep cool.

Thanks be to God for His unspeakable gift—
indescribable, inestimable, incomparable,
inexpressible—precious beyond words.

LOIS LEBAR

Reindeer Hay

1 (12 ounce) package butterscotch chips

1 (12 ounce) jar peanut butter

1 (9 ounce) can chow mein noodles

In saucepan, stir butterscotch chips over low heat until melted. Add peanut butter to chips and remove from heat. Stir well. Mix in chow mein noodles. Drop by teaspoonfuls onto wax paper. Allow to cool and set for at least 1 hour.

Reindeer Nibblers

1 package small pretzels
1 box rice cereal
1 can salted peanuts
Salt
Garlic salt

1 stick butter, melted
1½ tablespoons Worcestershire sauce
1½ tablespoons soy sauce

Put pretzels, cereal, and peanuts into roaster pan and toss to mix. Sprinkle with dash of salt and dash of garlic salt. Combine remaining ingredients and pour over mixture. Toss again and bake at 325 degrees for about 1 hour, stirring every 15 minutes.

Reindeer Sugar Cookies

1 teaspoon baking powder

1 teaspoon vanilla

½ teaspoon salt

1 cup sugar

¾ cup butter, softened (no substitutions)

2 eggs

2½ cups flour

Powdered sugar

Mix all ingredients except flour and powdered sugar. Slowly add flour until mixture forms a ball. For best results, chill for 30 minutes. Roll out on surface dusted with powdered sugar. Use reindeer cookie cutters. Place on greased cookie sheets. Bake at 350 degrees for about 8 minutes. Cool and decorate.

Reindeer Lunch

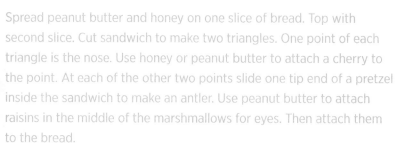

Peanut butter
Honey
Sandwich bread
Cherries

Pretzels
Raisins
Marshmallows

Spread peanut butter and honey on one slice of bread. Top with second slice. Cut sandwich to make two triangles. One point of each triangle is the nose. Use honey or peanut butter to attach a cherry to the point. At each of the other two points slide one tip end of a pretzel inside the sandwich to make an antler. Use peanut butter to attach raisins in the middle of the marshmallows for eyes. Then attach them to the bread.

Tell your children (young and old) about the real Saint Nicholas who lived long ago. He was a fourth-century saint who was known by his love for God and his secret gift giving. Research Saint Nick (the creators of VeggieTales have several fantastic movies about Saint Nick) as a family, and plan to do your own secret gift giving for someone in need this Christmas.

Saint Nick's Whiskers

1 cup butter
1 cup sugar
2 tablespoons milk
1 teaspoon vanilla

2½ cups flour
⅔ cup red candied cherries, finely chopped
½ cup finely chopped nuts
¾ cup flaked coconut

Cream together butter and sugar; blend in milk and vanilla. Stir in flour, candied cherries, and nuts. Form into 2 logs. Roll in coconut. Wrap and chill overnight. Slice and bake on ungreased cookie sheet at 375 degrees for 10 to 12 minutes.

The giver of every good and perfect gift has called upon us to mimic His giving, by grace, through faith, and this is not of ourselves.

THE REAL SAINT NICHOLAS

Prancer's Favorite Mix

1 (6 ounce) package semisweet
 chocolate chips

¼ cup vegetable oil

¼ cup creamy peanut butter

6 cups Crispix cereal

2 cups sugar

1 cup peanuts

1 cup raisins

1 cup red and green chocolate-
 coated candy pieces

Melt chocolate chips, oil, and peanut butter in microwave for 1 minute
at a time. Stir until fully melted. Add remaining ingredients and mix.
Place in greased 9x13-inch pan and cool completely. Break apart and
store in airtight container.

Reindeer Antlers

½ cup semisweet chocolate chips
½ cup milk chocolate chips
½ cup butterscotch chips

2 cups chow mein noodles
Maraschino cherries, halved

Line cookie sheet with wax paper. In saucepan, melt chocolate and butterscotch chips over low heat, stirring occasionally. Remove from heat and stir in chow mein noodles. With teaspoon, drop onto cookie sheet in a V pattern. Press cherry half into center of each cookie with cut side down. Chill in refrigerator until set.

Reindeer Punch

¼ cup sugar

3¼ cups water, divided

6 cups cranberry juice cocktail

1½ cups orange juice

Juice of 1 lemon

6 cups cranberry ginger ale (or regular ginger ale)

Cloves and orange slices for garnish

Dissolve sugar in ¼ cup warm water. Add remaining water and juice. Chill. Add ginger ale just before serving. Garnish with cloves and orange slices.

Saint Nick's Favorite Cookies

4½ cups flour, sifted
½ teaspoon salt
1 teaspoon baking soda
1½ cups sugar

1 cup butter (no substitutions)
¼ teaspoon almond extract
3 eggs
Pinch cinnamon

Sift together flour, salt, and soda and set aside. Cream together sugar, butter, almond extract, eggs, and cinnamon. Combine mixtures. Roll out dough ¼ inch thick. Cut into Christmas shapes. Place on ungreased cookie sheets and bake at 350 degrees for 8 to 10 minutes. Frost as desired.

Reindeer Graham Cookies

Graham cracker squares
1 can prepared chocolate frosting
Mini chocolate chips

Red cinnamon candies (or other red candy pieces)
Miniature pretzels, broken in half

Gently cut graham cracker squares diagonally in half. Spread a small amount of frosting over top side of cracker. Form a triangle head by topping with remaining cracker so the two narrow ends meet to form the reindeer's nose. Spread small amount of frosting to cover the top cracker. Use chocolate chips for eyes and cinnamon candy for nose. Add pretzel halves for antlers. Repeat until remaining ingredients have been used. Let set on wire rack.

Saint Nick Punch

1 quart cranberry juice
1 cup orange juice
1 cup pineapple juice
¼ cup lemon juice

½ cup sugar
2 cups chilled ginger ale
1 pint orange sherbet

Mix juices and sugar together. Add ginger ale, then sherbet. Stir gently.
Serve over ice or chill with ice ring made of cranberries and ginger ale.

Old Saint Nick Bread

A reindeer favorite!

2 eggs

¼ cup vegetable oil

1 cup sugar

1 cup milk

½ teaspoon salt

3¼ cups flour

3½ teaspoons baking powder

1 cup chopped peanuts

1 cup red and green gumdrops, chopped

Beat eggs, oil, and sugar until light and fluffy. Add milk and salt. Mix well. Add flour and baking powder. Fold in nuts and gumdrops. Spread in greased and floured loaf pan and bake at 350 degrees for 1 hour.

Rudolph's Drink

Cranberry juice   Ginger ale

Vanilla ice cream

Half fill a tall glass with cranberry juice. Add a big scoop of vanilla ice cream. Add enough ginger ale to float the ice cream.

Saint Nick's Minty Ice Cream Dream

20 chocolate sandwich cookies, crushed

½ stick butter, softened

½ gallon special edition peppermint ice cream

1 cup powdered sugar

6 ounces chocolate chips

5 ounces evaporated milk

½ stick butter

1 (8 ounce) container whipped topping

Chocolate sauce

Mix cookies and softened butter and press into 9x13-inch pan. Spread ice cream over cookie mixture and freeze for 2 hours. In saucepan over medium-high heat, mix sugar, chocolate chips, evaporated milk, and ½ stick butter until chips melt. Allow to cool. Pour and spread over frozen layers. Freeze for 2 or 3 more hours. Top with whipped topping and freeze. Defrost for 10 minutes before serving. Serve with chocolate sauce.

Mrs. Claus's Famous Brownies

2 (1 ounce) squares unsweetened chocolate
½ cup sugar
¼ cup shortening
2 eggs, beaten

½ cup flour
¼ teaspoon baking powder
¼ teaspoon salt
¾ cup chopped pecans
Whipped cream

Combine first 3 ingredients in saucepan and cook until chocolate is melted and mixture is smooth. Add eggs, beating well. Stir flour, baking powder, and salt into chocolate mixture until well blended. Mix in pecans. Turn into 9x9-inch pan lined with foil. Bake at 350 degrees for 40 minutes or until toothpick comes out clean. Cool and serve with whipped cream.

Elf Cookies

1 cup butter

¾ cup sugar

¾ cup brown sugar

1 egg

2 cups flour

1 teaspoon soda

½ teaspoon salt

1 teaspoon cinnamon

1 teaspoon nutmeg

½ teaspoon cloves

1 cup rolled oats

Combine all ingredients. Roll into very small balls; flatten with floured glass on greased cookie sheet. Bake at 350 degrees for 15 minutes.

Jolly Old Saint Nick's Gelatin

2 large boxes lime gelatin   8 ounces vanilla yogurt

Mix lime gelatin according to package directions. Set half aside. Place other half in Christmas mold or Bundt cake pan. Let set completely in fridge. Meanwhile, add yogurt to remaining gelatin and set aside at room temperature. When gelatin in fridge has set, take out and pour gelatin and yogurt mixture on top. Refrigerate until set.

Nogs & Logs

*Faith expects from God what
is beyond all expectation.*

ANDREW MURRAY

Christmas Log Cookies

¾ cup sugar

¾ cup brown sugar

½ cup shortening

½ cup butter (no substitutions)

1 egg, beaten

2 cups flour

1 teaspoon cinnamon

½ teaspoon allspice

½ teaspoon nutmeg

½ teaspoon ground cloves

½ teaspoon baking soda

½ teaspoon baking powder

Mix all ingredients and shape into log. Chill. Slice and bake at 350 degrees for 10 minutes. After baking, sprinkle with sugar.

Hot Chocolate

1 (1 pound) can powdered
   chocolate drink mix
1 pound sugar

1 (8 ounce) box powdered sugar
1 (3 to 6 ounce) jar powdered
   creamer

Sift all ingredients. Store in airtight container. For each mug of hot
chocolate, add 4 heaping teaspoons of mixture to 1 cup boiling water.

Snowy Cinnamon Cocoa

4 cups milk
1 cup chocolate syrup
1 teaspoon cinnamon

Frozen whipped topping, thawed
¼ cup semisweet chocolate chips

Place milk and chocolate syrup in microwave-safe bowl and stir. Cook on high for 3 to 4 minutes or until hot. Stir in cinnamon. Pour into 4 large mugs and garnish with whipped topping and chocolate chips.

The Ultimate Chocolate Chip Bar

1 cup butter, melted

1 cup brown sugar

1 cup sugar

2 eggs

1 teaspoon vanilla

2 cups flour

½ teaspoon salt

1 teaspoon baking soda

½ teaspoon baking powder

2 cups quick oats

12 ounces semisweet chocolate chips

In large bowl, mix ingredients in order given; spread in greased 9x13-inch pan. Bake at 350 degrees for 20 to 25 minutes. Cool and cut into squares.

Gail's Yuletide Layer Bars

½ cup butter

2½ cups graham cracker crumbs

1½ cups chopped nuts

1½ cups flaked coconut

1 (10 ounce) package chocolate chips with holiday shapes and morsels

1 (14 ounce) can sweetened condensed milk

Preheat oven to 350 degrees. Melt butter in 9x13-inch baking pan in oven. Remove from oven. Sprinkle graham cracker crumbs over butter; stir well. Press onto bottom of pan. Sprinkle with nuts, coconut, and chocolate chips. Pour condensed milk evenly over top. Bake for 25 to 30 minutes or until light golden brown. Cool completely in pan on wire rack.

Fudge Logs

1½ cups semisweet chocolate chips
1½ cups butterscotch chips

7 ounces sweetened condensed milk
½ teaspoon vanilla

Melt chocolate chips, butterscotch chips, and milk in saucepan over low heat, stirring until smooth. Remove from heat and stir in vanilla. Pour into 8x8-inch pan and refrigerate until firm. Cut into 1-inch logs.

Leah's Apple-Cranberry Cider

2 quarts apple cider or juice

4 cups cranberry juice

Juice of 2 freshly squeezed
 oranges

⅔ cup packed brown sugar

8 whole cloves

4 cinnamon sticks

In large saucepan, combine cider, cranberry juice, orange juice, and brown sugar. Place cloves and cinnamon sticks in cheesecloth and tie with string; place in saucepan. Bring to a boil over medium heat; reduce heat and simmer on low for 20 minutes. Discard spice bag before serving.

This is Christmas: not the tinsel,
not the giving and receiving, not even
the carols, but the humble heart that
receives anew the wondrous gift, the Christ.

FRANK MCKIBBEN

Cinnamon Cider

1 quart apple cider   ¼ cup red hot cinnamon candies

Pour apple cider into large pot and add cinnamon candies. Heat and
stir until candies melt and cider turns red. Pour into mugs and serve
while hot.

Holiday Punch

½ gallon lime or raspberry sherbet   2 quarts ginger ale or other clear
                                                                        soda pop

Scoop sherbet into punch bowl. Slowly pour ginger ale over sherbet.
Serve cold.

Seven-Layer Bars

½ cup butter

1 cup graham cracker crumbs

1 cup semisweet chocolate chips

1 cup butterscotch chips

½ to 1 cup chopped nuts

1 cup flaked coconut

1 (14 ounce) can sweetened
condensed milk

In 9x13-inch pan, cut butter and melt in 350-degree oven to coat bottom. Sprinkle graham cracker crumbs on top. Pat down. Sprinkle chocolate and butterscotch chips, nuts, and coconut on top. Drizzle milk evenly over all. Bake for 30 minutes or until lightly browned.

Traditional Eggnog

4 eggs, separated
½ cup sugar, divided
2 cups cold milk
1 cup cold light cream

1½ teaspoons vanilla
⅛ teaspoon salt
¼ teaspoon nutmeg

Beat egg yolks and ¼ cup sugar until thick. Gradually mix in milk, cream, vanilla, salt, and nutmeg, beating until frothy. Beat egg whites with remaining ¼ cup sugar until mixture forms soft peaks; fold into egg yolk mixture. Cover and chill. Mix well before serving and sprinkle with nutmeg.

If you're preparing traditional eggnog with raw eggs, make sure to buy them local from a farmers' market where you know exactly where they came from and how old they are Only buy fresh eggs for eggnog. To play it safe, use our Festive Eggless Eggnog recipe (on page 151) or buy the pasteurized eggnog from the grocery store!

Festive Eggless Eggnog

8 cups whole milk, divided

1 (3 ounce) package vanilla instant pudding

½ cup sugar

2 teaspoons vanilla

½ teaspoon nutmeg

Dash cinnamon

In large bowl, mix pudding mix with 1 cup milk. When pudding is thick, add remaining ingredients and mix well. Chill and serve.

Parrish Christmas Punch

1 quart strawberry sherbet

1 quart lemon-lime soda

1 quart ginger ale

1 small can frozen pink lemonade concentrate, thawed

Blend all ingredients and serve with a garnish of fresh mint.

Donna's Christmas Punch

1 (12 ounce) can frozen grape juice
  concentrate, thawed

1 (6 ounce) can frozen cranberry
  cocktail juice concentrate,
  thawed

2 cups orange juice

1 (2 liter) bottle lemon-lime soda

Orange or lemon slices

Mix first 4 ingredients in punch bowl and garnish with orange or lemon slices. Add ice ring or crushed ice. Depending on the number of people at your holiday celebration, you may want to double the recipe.

Christmas Cereal Bars

½ cup margarine

1 bag large marshmallows

½ cup creamy peanut butter

½ cup raisins

4 cups toasted oats cereal

Red and green chocolate-coated candy pieces

Melt margarine over low heat in deep saucepan. Stir in marshmallows until smooth and creamy. Mix in peanut butter. Remove from heat; add raisins, cereal, and chocolate candies, stirring until evenly coated. With buttered hands, press mixture into 9x13-inch pan. Cool; cut into bars.

Kids' Favorite Christmas Punch

1 small can frozen orange juice concentrate, thawed

1 small can frozen lemonade concentrate, thawed

1 envelope strawberry Kool-Aid (unsweetened)

1 envelope cherry Kool-Aid (unsweetened)

1 tall can tropical fruit punch

2 (12 ounce) cans ginger ale

Prepare orange juice and lemonade according to directions on cans. Add Kool-Aid, using half amount of water and 2 cups sugar required. Add tropical fruit punch. Pour into punch bowl; add ginger ale and ice cubes.

More light than we can learn,
More wealth than we can treasure,
More love than we can earn,
More peace than we can measure,
Because one Child is born.

CHRISTOPHER FRY

Wassail

2 quarts apple cider
2 (14 ounce) cans pineapple juice
2 cups orange juice
1 cup lemon juice

1 stick whole cinnamon
1 teaspoon whole cloves
1 cup sugar

Combine all ingredients in large pot and simmer for 5 minutes. Strain and refrigerate overnight. Reheat and serve warm.

Recipe Index